FUN THINGS TO MAKE AND DO FOR EIGHT YEAR OLDS.

FUN
THINGS TO MAKE
AND DO FOR

8

YEAR OLDS

Irene Newington

Illustrated by Ian McGee

RED FOX

A Red Fox Book

Published by Random Century Children's Books
20 Vauxhall Bridge Road, London SW1V 2SA
A division of the Random Century Group

London Melbourne Sydney Auckland
Johannesburg and agencies throughout the world

First published 1991

Set in Plantin
Typeset by JH Graphics Ltd, Reading

Printed and bound in Great Britain by
Cox & Wyman Ltd, Reading, Berkshire

ISBN 0 09 974600 X

Contents

Tips to Help You   7
Merry Go Round   9
Dachshund Dog   11

Mini Furniture   14
Oliver Owl   18

Theatre and Play Figures   22
Ball Pet   24
Fish Wind Chime   28
Box Loom   30
Peepshow   34
Roses All The Way   37
Flower Cart   44
Windmill   47
Sammy Spider   49

Victorian Ribbon Plate   51
Treasure Island   53
Glove Kitten   55
Sally Spoon Puppet   58
Clipboard for Your Notes   62
Light as Air Paper Ball Decorations   65
Lollipop Rabbit Easter Card   67
Wooden Easter Eggs   70
Ball Head Clown   72

Window Box Card   75
Black Cat for Hallowe'en   77
Tea Party Plate   79
Newspaper Figures   83
Two Christmas Lanterns   85
Peacock Wall Mural   88
Christmas Decoration, Christmas Calendar   91
Woody Woodpecker   93

Tips to Help You

Collect useful little bits such as buttons, sequins, matchboxes, pipecleaners, silver paper.

Keep your collection in separate containers so that you can find everything easily.

Be a neat worker, clear up after yourself. Put all the tools away.

If you are not sure, try to draw out your idea on paper first.

Use a template (a piece of card cut into a shape) for shapes where you need more than one the same. It is easy to get left and right shapes then.

Cover your work space with newspaper, cover your clothes with an apron.

To see if a model will stand up when it is made from paper, you can check the strength of the paper by balancing a coin on the corner.

 Straws glued together make good tube shapes.

Wobbly model legs will stand better if you fold them slightly down the middle.

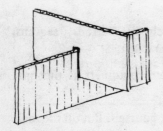

Corrugated card cuts easily and also slots together well.

Remember scissors and needles are sharp! Before cutting from the middle of a piece of paper, fold it first.

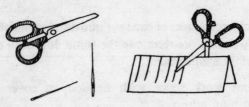

Good drawing pencils are called 2B.

Parts of a circle

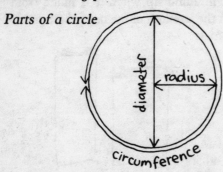

Both Blu-Tack and Plasticine are useful for holding bits in place, and they are less messy than Sellotape.

Merry Go Round

You need:

Large size cheese box and lid, cardboard, 5
straws, 1 pipe cleaner, Sellotape, split pin,
scissors, felt tip pens.

What to do

1 Put the cheese box lid upside down on top of its box.
2 Poke a hole right in the middle of the box and the lid.
Push a split pin through the hole and open it out at the
back. This allows the box to turn round and round.

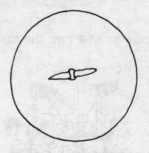

3 Draw five roundabout
horse shapes on card.
Colour them in and cut
them out.

4 Sellotape a straw across the middle of each horse (pointing upwards).

5 Sellotape the straw ends on to the INSIDE of the roundabout circle.

6 Cut five flag shapes and glue them on to the top of the straws.

7 Sellotape a pipe cleaner handle on to the side to turn the roundabout.

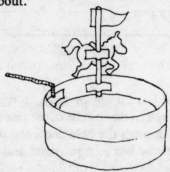

8 Put some music on and turn the roundabout round and round.

Dachshund Dog

This cheerful little chap comes complete with collar and lead.

You need:

Kitchen roll, tissue paper, lolly stick, cardboard, 4 large beads, felt tip pens, 1 small black bead, glue, 2 black buttons, ribbon, bits of felt (black and red).

What to do

1 Cut two-thirds of the roll off for the body.

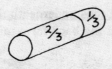

2 Colour this piece in brown and black and fill with tissue paper.
3 Use the remaining third for the head; colour as for the body and fill it with tissue paper.
4 Cut two ear shapes and glue them on to the top of the head.

5   Glue on two black buttons for eyes and a black bead for a nose. Use a tiny bit of red felt for the tongue.

6   Poke a hole in the top of the body and underneath the head. Put a dab of glue at each end of the stick and push it into the holes to join the head to the body.

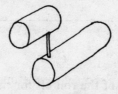

7   Glue four large beads underneath the body, and glue a tiny strip of felt at the back for a tail.

8   Tie a ribbon round Dachshund dog's neck for a collar.
9   Make a lead for your dog (see next page).

Lead for Dachshund Dog

These kinds of braid are very useful for other things too: bag handles, mats, toys.

> **You need:**
> Thick wool, pencil.

What to do

1 Get a VERY LONG piece of thick wool (at least 3 feet long).
2 Knot both ends together.
3 Loop one end over a door handle and the other end over a pencil. Pull tight and twist the pencil round and round.

4 When all the wool is fully twisted take the pencil to the handle. The two ends of twisted wool will coil together. Pull both pieces of twisted wool through your hand to smooth out any tangles.
5 Take out the pencil, remove the twisted braid from the door handle and tie a knot in the end.

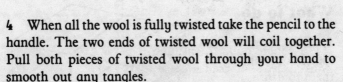

Mini Furniture

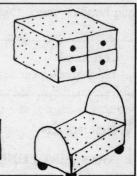

Chest of drawers

You need:
4 matchboxes, glue, split pins, material or fablon.

What to do

1 Glue together four
matchboxes and leave
them to dry.

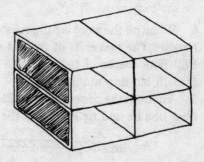

2 Take out the matchbox trays. Poke a hole in the front of each tray, push a split pin through and press it flat at the back.

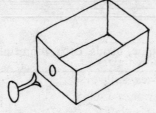

3 Cover the outside of the chest with a little fablon or material and put the trays back in.

Table

You need:
Small, round cheese box, matchbox, glue.

What to do

1 Glue the round box on top of the matchbox.

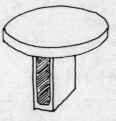

2 Cut a circle of thin material larger than the round box.
Place a dab of glue in the middle and put the material on the table for a cloth.

Bed

> **You need:**
> 4 matchboxes, glue, beads, card, material.

What to do

1   Glue together four matchboxes (see picture) and leave them to dry.
2   Measure the box ends, and cut two semicircle shapes to that size.
3   Glue one at the top and one at the bottom.
4   Glue four beads underneath for legs.
5   Cut out some scraps of material for bedding.

Easy chair

> **You need:**
> 5 matchboxes, material or fablon, glue, 4 beads.

What to do

1 Glue together two matchboxes for the seat.
2 Cover them with fablon, or glue material over them.

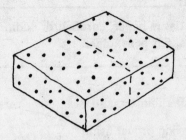

3 Do the same with three other matchboxes, then glue these on to the seat for the arms and back.
4 Glue four small beads underneath for legs.

Oliver Owl

What to do

1 Colour the bag brown using feathery strokes.

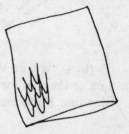

2 Cut two feet shapes out of card.

3 Cut out a circle of card for the base. To make a good circle draw round a cup or saucer.

4 Cut two large circles of a light-coloured felt and two small circles of darker felt for the eyes. Glue the small ones on to the larger ones.

5 Cut out a triangle shape for the beak. Fold it down the middle and colour it in.

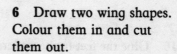

6 Draw two wing shapes. Colour them in and cut them out.

7   Stuff the bird's body (the bag) with tissue paper until it is nice and plump: be careful not to tear it. Pull up the bag corners for ears.

8   With some scissors, clip the edges of the opening of the bag all round about 1 cm apart. Dab these with glue and press them down on to the circle. Leave it to dry.

9   Glue on the eyes and the beak. Glue the wings to the sides.

10   Glue the feet to the underside of the base, so that the wide part of the feet and the claws stick out from underneath.

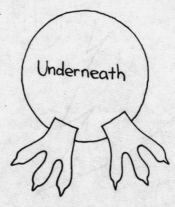

11 Make a perch for your owl by rolling a piece of corrugated card into a tube shape. Glue the edges and leave it to dry. Perch your owl on top.

Theatre and Play Figures

Victorian children used to play with this kind of theatre.

You need:

Large shallow cardboard grocery box, card,
powder paint, scissors, drawing paper, Sellotape,
glue, straws, pipe cleaners, bits of material.

What to do

1 Use a grocery box for the theatre. Cut off the lid and
turn the box on its side. Mix some powder paint and paint
the outside of the box.

2 Ask someone to cut two
long slits in both sides of the
box (see the picture).

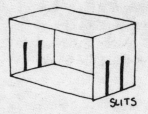

3 Decide which story you
want to act out and paint a
scene for a background on to
a piece of paper. Glue or
Sellotape the scenery on to
the back of the box.

4 Hang two narrow lengths of material at the front of the box for curtains. Attach them to the top with glue or staples.

5 Cut out a piece of rectangular card. Fold the bottom third of the card back to make a stand and draw a figure on to the rest. Colour the figures in and cut them out, leaving the folded part at the bottom for each one to stand on.

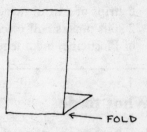

← FOLD

6 Glue a pipe cleaner or wooden spill on to the back of each figure.

7 When your figures are finished put them in the theatre and draw the pipe cleaners or spills through the slits in the sides so that you can move them about the stage.

8 Make up a play and act it out, moving the figures and speaking the words.

Ball Pet

You need:

6 strips of stiff drawing paper, 25 cm × 3 cm.
2 split pins, small piece of card, felt tip pens, bit
of Plasticine, 6 cm length of wool.

What to do

1 Decorate the strips of
paper with a colourful
design.

2 Put the six strips with their ends overlapping to form
a star shape as in the picture.

3 Put a split pin through all six strips at the centre point
where they overlap and press the star flat.

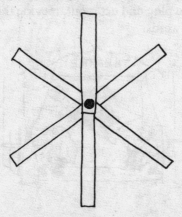

4   Take the other end of each strip, join them together in the same way and fasten them together with another split pin. Now you have a ball shape.

5   Make a pet shape to put in the ball (look for some shapes to use on pp. 26–27). Draw or trace the shape, colour it in on both sides and cut it out.

6   Hang the bird shape from the inside of the roof of the ball. Fix the rabbit or mouse on to the base with a small piece of Plasticine.

7   Tie a piece of wool to the top of the ball and hang it up.

Some Pet Shapes

Fish Wind Chime

You need:

Strips of drawing paper, ruler, pencil, felt tip pens, milk bottle tops, sequins, cotton, needle, scissors, glue, stapler.

What to do

1 Measure and cut out two strips of drawing paper measuring 30 cm × 2 cm.

2 Place one strip on top of the other and staple them together at the end. Push them out to make an oval shape and staple the other end about a quarter of the total length in.

3 Place two more strips of paper around the first two. Bend them out further and staple them in the same place. This time you won't have so much paper left at the end. Curl the end bits of paper outwards to make a tail shape.

4   Cut three more strips of paper 25cm × 2cm. Curl them into a loose spiral shape and glue the ends.

5   Glue the spirals to the inner oval of the fish shape. Paint the fish in fishy colours or stick sequins on the strips to imitate scales.

6   Poke a hole in the top of the fish and push a thread through (you could use a threaded needle). Knot the thread on the inside of the strip of paper so it stays in place. This is to hang the fish up with.

7   Poke three holes at equal distances apart along the bottom of the fish.

8   Take three lengths of cotton and thread bottle tops on to each length. Tie the threads through the holes at the bottom of the fish.

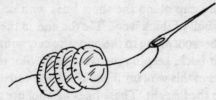

9   Hang your wind chime up by a window to blow in a breeze.

Box Loom

What to do

1 Draw short lines one centimetre apart along both ends
of the shoe box.

2 Carefully clip along the short lines with scissors.

3 Take a ball of thick wool. Tie the end to the first cut,
then take the wool along to the opposite cut, wrap it round
and bring it back, keeping the wool tight. Slot the thread
into the cuts in this way until you reach the end of the box.
Tie it off in the last slit. These lines of wool are called the
WARP.

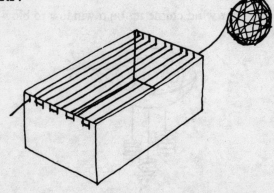

4 Thread a long piece of wool through a large needle
(double the wool up if you like). Start at the first line of

WARP and take your needle under and over each line. At the end turn and take the needle back along the lines, going over and under. When you reach the end of your wool, tie it and start again from where you left off with a new length.

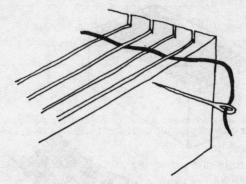

5 Push the lines of weaving together with a comb. These lines are called the WEFT. Try weaving different coloured stripes for an interesting effect.

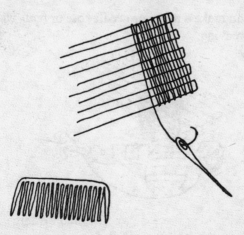

6   When all the warp is covered and you have a full piece of weaving, slip the weaving off the loom by lifting it out of the slits on the box. If you are careful you can use the loom again.

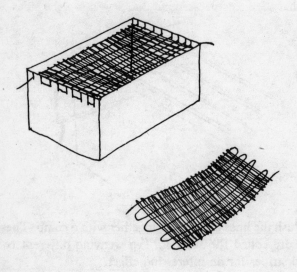

7   You can make a purse or needle case or mats with the piece of weaving.

Purse

1 Fold the piece of weaving and sew down the sides.

2 Stitch on a button and a loop (as shown).

Needle case

Place a small piece of material on top of the weaving and sew down the middle. Fold over. Keep the needles inside by sticking them through the material.

Peepshow

You need:

Shoebox, greaseproof paper, drawing paper, Sellotape, felt tip pens, scissors.

What to do

1 Colour a scene all round inside the shoe box. It could be a wood or a sea scene, anything you like.
2 Poke a small round hole in one end of the box and cut a little square hole in the side of the box at the other end at the top.

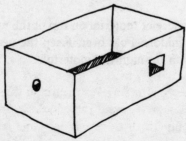

3 Draw some figures for your scene on card this shape with a tab folded back (see p. 36).

4 Put some glue on your figure tabs and fix them on to the floor of the box.

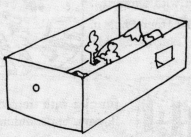

5 Put greaseproof paper over the top of the box to make a lid and Sellotape it round the edges.

6 Look through the little round peephole into the scene. The scene looks even better if you shine a torch through the square side window. Try Sellotaping a tiny piece of coloured cellophane (toffee paper) over the square window, and then shining the torch through. You could do a night scene with dark blue paper over the hole or a sandy desert scene with yellow paper to give a hot feel.

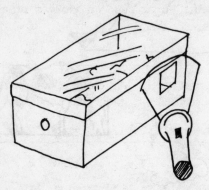

Scene ideas

Underwater: with seaweed, shipwreck, fish, octopus, shells.

Jungle: with tropical trees, flowers, birds, animals.

Favourite scene: a scene from a story you like.

Roses All The Way

Enjoy collecting rose petals and any scented herbs during the warm summer days. You can make a number of scented delights with them.

You need:

Bowl or jar, rose petals, salt, cloth, spoon, orris root powder, scented oil, small jars, paper, ribbons.

Pot-pourri

You need:
Rose petals, drawing paper, salt, scraps of pretty material, jar or bowl, spoon, felt pens, small bottles/containers, orris root powder, scented oils (which can be bought at a health shop or a herb shop).

What to do

1 Place a layer of rose petals in a large bowl or jar. Sprinkle some salt over them. Do this again and again with thin layers of petals and salt until the bowl if full.

2 Cover the bowl and leave it for ten days in a dark, airy place.

3 Stir the mixture with a spoon and scatter some orris root powder on top. Add a few drops of scented oil (this is strong smelling so use only a few drops). Stir the petals and mix it together well, then cover the bowl and leave it for a few hours.

4 This scented, dried mixture is called pot-pourri pronounced like 'poe-pourry' and is lovely for scenting rooms. Keep some in a nice bowl and it will make the whole room smell good. You could also make Christmas or birthday presents out of it by putting the pot-pourri into small, pretty jars. Attach a label, and decorate the jar with ribbons and you have lovely presents to give away.

Collect all kinds of small jars and containers ready for your scented presents.

Label suggestions

Scented waters

Keep an eye open for small, pretty glass bottles, and plastic containers in junk shops or markets, perfect for scented waters.

You need:
Rose petals to fill a $\frac{1}{2}$-litre (1-pint) jug, herbs such as thyme, lavender or lemon balm, (all easy herbs to grow or buy), hot water. (ASK SOMEONE TO HELP YOU WITH THE HOT WATER.)*

What to do

1   Put the rose petals (and the herbs if you are using them) in a jug. Pour in enough HOT* water to fill the jug. Leave it to cool.

2   While the scented water is cooling, make some pretty labels on drawing paper to tie around the bottle necks (see above).

3   Pour the cooled liquid through a strainer or sieve into another jug, and then pour the strained liquid into the bottles.

4   Tie your labels on with ribbon.

Pressed roses

You need:
Rose petals, blotting paper, book, card.

What to do

1 Put separate rose petals between blotting paper. Place this under a heavy book and leave for a couple of weeks. Use the pressed roses to decorate cards or gift tags.
2 Put the cards in a box with some of your pot-pourri and you will have lovely scented cards to give away or send to friends at Christmas or their birthdays.

Bags of perfume

You need:
Scraps of pretty material 18 cm × 12 cm, needle and thread, pot-pourri, ribbon.

1   Fold each piece of material in half and sew them into bags.

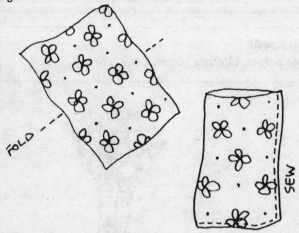

2   Fill the bags with your rose pot-pourri (see p. 37 for how to make it) and tie them at the top with a ribbon.
3   These make lovely presents, especially for older people like grandmothers, to keep in clothes cupboards, drawers and among their writing paper.

Bath sachets

You need:
Scraps of pretty material 18 cm × 12 cm, needle
and thread, pot-pourri, ribbon.

1   Make bags in the same way as the perfume bags.
2   Fill them with the pot-pourri mixture and tie them
closed with a LONG ribbon.
3   When you next have a bath, hang these bags under the
running warm water tap to release the perfume, giving
you lovely scented bath water.

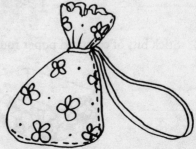

Flower Cart

If you have made the pot-pourri in this book, put some of it in with your flowers.

You need:

Teabag box, cardboard, coloured tissue paper, felt pens, Sellotape, scissors, 2 split pins.

What to do

1 Cut the lid off the teabox (save the lid).

2 Stick bits of coloured paper round the box to decorate it.

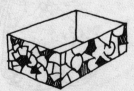

3 Draw two circles on the card
for wheels and cut them out.

4 Make a hole in the middle of each wheel and on each
side of the box. Push a split pin through each wheel.

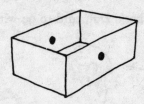

5 Push one of the split pins through the hole in one of
the cart sides, and the other pin through the opposite hole.
Open the pin out at the back.

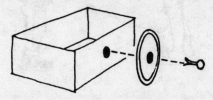

6 Cut two handle shapes from the lid of the box and glue
them on to the cart.

7   Fill the cart with a mound of green tissue paper.
8   Cut lots of flower shapes from coloured tissue paper and glue them on to the green mound.

9   Make a Mother's Day card to go with it.

Windmill

You need:

Yoghurt pot, cardboard, thin nail, small cork,
scissors, felt pens.

What to do

1 Draw two sail shapes on the card and cut them out.
Colour them in.

2 Cross the sails and ask someone to push a thin nail
through the middle.

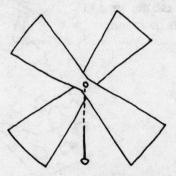

3   Make a hole in the side at the top of the pot.
4   Push the nail through the hole and ask someone to press a small cork on to the back of the nail inside the pot. This holds the sails in place and lets them spin round. Twist each half of the sails slightly sideways, so that it will catch the wind.

5   Cut out a card door and glue it on.
6   On a piece of card glue a mound of green tissue paper to make a hill. Glue the windmill on top of the hill.
7   Make some small model animals and place them at the foot of the hill.
8   On a windy way take the windmill into the garden and watch the sails go round.

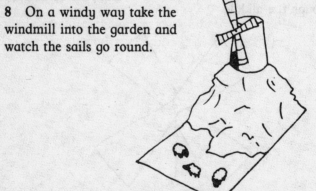

Sammy Spider

What to do

1 Use one section of a cardboard egg box to make the body.

2 Paint or colour this black and leave it to dry.

3 Get someone to help you to poke four holes in the top of the cup around the sides.

4 Push a pipe cleaner into each hole and twist the bit inside into a knot to stop it coming out again.

5 Put a small bead on the end of each leg and squeeze the pipe cleaner over the bead.

6 Cut out two circles of paper and glue them on the body for eyes. Glue two small beads into the middle of the spider's eyes.

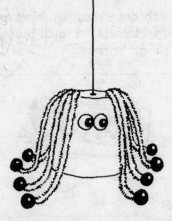

7 Make a hole in the top of the spider's body and thread through a piece of thin elastic.

8 Suspend Sammy Spider from the ceiling or in front of the window and bounce him up and down.

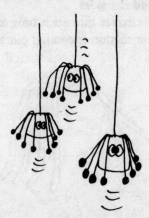

Victorian Ribbon Plate

An easy-to-make present as a special gift. Save pictures from Christmas or birthday cards.

You need:

White paper plate, ribbon or thick wool, ruler, felt pens, needle, beads or sequins, glue.

What to do

1 Either draw a picture or glue one on to the middle of the plate. An old-fashioned scene, flowers or animals is best. If you're not very good at drawing, cut one out of a magazine.

2 Using the width of a ruler to measure the spacing, mark lines all round the edge of the plate. Get someone to help you carefully to push scissors into the marks and clip along the lines to make slots.

SLOTS

3   Starting at the bottom of the plate, thread a long piece of ribbon or wool in and out of the slots.

4   A large-eyed needle would help you thread the ribbon through. Go round the plate three times, leave a short tail each time.

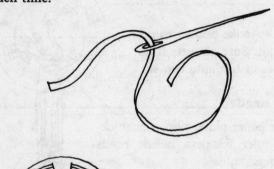

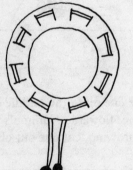

5   Glue the sequins between the ribbon spaces and thread the beads on to the ends of the tails.

6   Sellotape a loop of ribbon to the back of the plate so that you can hang it up.

Treasure Island

A box to keep your treasures in.

You need:

Cardboard egg box, scissors, shells, tissue paper, card, drawing paper, felt tip pens, glue, brown paint or crayons.

What to do

1 Paint or colour the egg box to make it look like a rock. Open it out and leave to dry.

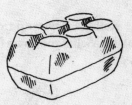

2 Take a piece of card big enough to sit the egg box on. Colour it in like the sea: blue, green, grey, white. Glue some shells round the edge.

3 Close the egg box up and glue the egg box rock on to the sea at one end.

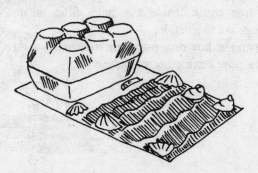

4   Colour a piece of paper 15 cm × 15 cm brown on one half and green on the other half. Colour the other side all green.

5   Cut a fringe into the half that is green on both sides.

6   Roll the paper up tightly with the brown part on the outside. Sellotape down the edge and frill out the top of the tree.

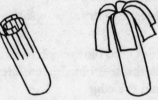

7   Poke a hole in the top of the egg box rock and push the palm tree trunk inside the hole. Stick it down with Sellotape on the inside.

8   Open the box and put your treasures in. You now have a secret hiding place.

Glove Kitten

Make two or three cuddly kittens and you will have a family of kittens.

You need:

Lady's glove, buttons, sequins, bell, ribbon, needle, wool, cotton wool, bits of felt, glue.

What to do

1 Stuff the glove with cotton wool right into each finger — make the body quite fat. Sew up the top (this will be the head). Pull it into shape so that four fingers become the legs and one sticks out at the end for the tail.

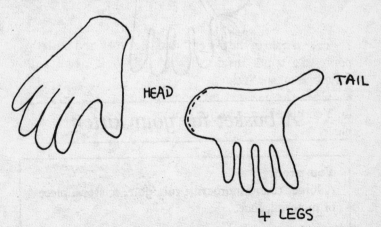

HEAD

TAIL

4 LEGS

2   Cut out two ear shapes from felt and sew them on to the top.

3   Tie a ribbon round the neck.

4   Stick on buttons for eyes and a piece of felt for a nose.

5   Sew some long pieces of wool on to the kitten's head.

6   Stick or sew some sequins on the kitten's body. You could also tie a bell on the ribbon.

A basket for your kitten

You need:
A large, round margarine tub, glue, scissors, piece of material, lace.

What to do

1 Make sure the tub is clean and dry.

2 Draw round the top of the tub on to the material; cut out the circle, leaving a space 3 cm all round.

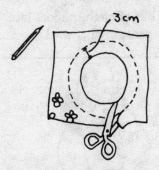

3 Glue all over inside the tub. Press in the material circle and leave the glue to dry.

4 Glue a length of lace all round the top edge of the tub.

Sally Spoon Puppet

Two or three puppets are enough for a little play.

You need:

Wooden spoon, bits of cloth, ribbon, lace, cardboard, glue, felt pens, needle, wool.

What to do

1 Colour a cheerful face on the back of the spoon.

2 Get a piece of cloth for the dress.

3 Sew small stitches along the top edge. Knot one end of the thread and leave the other end hanging.

4 Sew a piece of lace round the bottom of the dress.

5 Put the dress round the neck of the spoon, pull the stitches up tight and tie the thread tightly.

6   Glue a piece of lace around the neck.

7   Glue some wool on the bowl part of the spoon for hair, and fix a little hair at the front to make a fringe. Tie a ribbon in the puppet's hair.

8   Cut out two cardboard arms and glue them to the dress.

9 Hold the wooden handle underneath the dress so that your hand is hidden.

10 Go behind a table, kneel down and let your puppet dance on the stage.

Clipboard for Your Notes

You need:

1 piece of really strong card 24 cm × 30 cm,
wrapping paper, glue, bulldog clip, pencil, string
30 cm long, ruler.

What to do

1 Place the cardboard on the BACK of a piece of
wrapping paper.
2 Leave an edge all the way round.

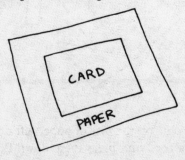

3 Draw a line all round the card, take off the card and glue the space left in the middle.
4 Put the card back on the glued area and press it down.
5 Leave it to dry under a heavy book.

6 When it has dried, take your sheet and place your ruler across each corner of the wrapping and draw a line just touching the corner of the card.
7 Cut off that corner (see the picture).

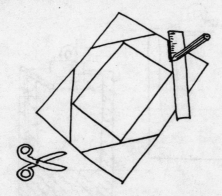

8 Put some glue on the bits of paper left and fold them over on to the card and press them down flat.

9 Let the board dry. The other side is the front of the board. Tie a piece of string 30 cm long to the end of a pencil.

10 Get someone to help you to poke a small, neat hole in the top corner of the board.

11 Tie the other end of the string to the board through the hole.

12 Fix the bulldog clip to the top edge of the board and slide the pencil through the top of the clip for safe keeping. Clip some sheets of paper to the board.

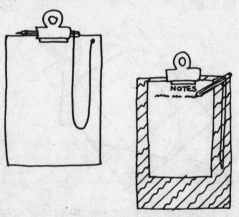

13 Now you can be a reporter and take notes.

Light as Air Paper Ball Decorations

These make good decorations for Christmas or a party.

You need:

12 tissue paper circles (if tissue paper not available, use thin paper), needle, cotton, silver stars or sequins, glue.

What to do

1 Fold each circle into quarters.

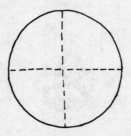

2 Thread a needle with cotton, and tie a knot in the other end.

3 Poke a hole in the top corner of each folded circle.

4 Put the needle through each hole until all twelve folded circles are on the cotton. Tie another knot in the thread the other side of the circles. Make it as tight as you can.

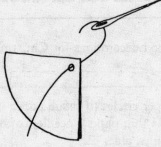

5 Open out the folded circles and twist them into a ball shape.

6 Put a dab of glue here and there and stick on silver stars or sequins.

7 Hang them up on threads.

Lollipop Rabbit Easter Card

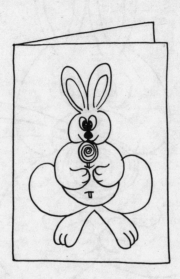

You need:

Stiff drawing paper, felt tip pens, scissors, 1
lollipop, buttons or felt, Sellotape.

What to do

1   Use a piece of stiff drawing paper 24 cm × 15 cm, fold
in half so that the card is now 12 cm × 15 cm.
2   Draw a rabbit on the front. (Look on the next page for
the shape.)

3 Colour the rabbit brightly for Easter.
4 Stick on buttons or circles of felt for the eyes.
5 Make two slits between the rabbit's paws, and thread the lollipop stick between the slits.
6 Write HAPPY EASTER inside your card.

HaPPY Easter
to YOU!

Easter Greetings!

HaPPY
Easter

Wooden Easter Eggs

You need:

Small flat pieces of balsa wood, glue, felt tip pens, ribbon, wool, scissors, small beads/toffee paper, needle and cotton.

What to do

1 First of all make a template in card of an egg shape.
2 Cut the shape out and use it to draw round.

3 Place the template on the balsa wood (you can buy balsa wood at a hobbies shop) and draw round it.
4 VERY CAREFULLY, A SNIP AT A TIME, cut the balsa wood egg shape out.

5 Decorate the eggs with lovely bright patterns, and glue on small beads and bits of shiny paper.

6 Thread a needle and GENTLY push the needle through near the top of the egg.

7 Tie a loop in the cotton.

8 To display your eggs, get a large twig and paint it white.

9 Put the twig in a plant pot full of soil and hang your eggs from its branches.

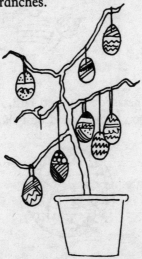

Ball Head Clown

A jazzy clown to sit in your bedroom.

You need:

Newspaper, white tissue paper, glue, 3 large
circles of coloured tissue, buttons, scraps of felt,
ribbon, sequins, scissors, drawing paper, cotton,
felt pens, Sellotape.

What to do

1 Squeeze the newspaper into a ball, and bind it with
Sellotape until you have a good ball shape.

2 Put the ball in the middle of the white tissue and wrap the tissue around it. Tie round the ends of the tissue with cotton, and pull out the edges like a collar.

TIE

3 Glue scraps of felt on for hair.

4 Stick buttons on for the eyes and nose and draw on a clown's mouth.

5 Stick three sequins on each cheek.

6 Cut out three LARGE circles of coloured tissue paper, each one slightly bigger than the other.

7 Put dabs of glue round the edges and decorate with sequins or glitter and leave to dry.

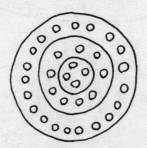

8 Put a dab of glue in the middle of each circle and stick one on top of the other in order of size.

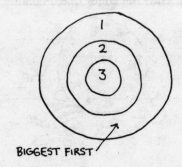

BIGGEST FIRST

9 Glue the clown's collar underneath and stick it on top of the top circle; lift up the edges of the collar.

Window Box Card

You need:

Stiff drawing paper, corrugated card, felt tip pens, scissors, glue, ruler.

What to do

1   Use a piece of drawing paper 28 cm × 16 cm.
2   Fold the paper over, now it is 14 cm × 16 cm.

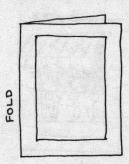

3   On the front draw a rectangle leaving about 3 cm all round the edges.
4   At the bottom of the rectangle draw some flowers.
5   Draw a line above the flowers.

6   Cut along this line and up the sides of the rectangle; raise this piece for the blind.

7   Cut out the space above the flowers around the outline of the flowers.

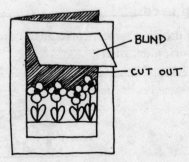

8   Glue a small piece of corrugated card below the flowers for the window box.

9   Colour in the blind in stripes and fold down the edge. You could cut the edges into a scalloped shape like in our picture.

10   Write a greeting in your card.

Black Cat
for Hallowe'en

You need:

Stiff drawing paper, black paper, crayons,
scissors, glue, silver stars, 2 green sequins.

What to do

1 Get a piece of drawing paper 28 cm × 16 cm. Fold it
in half, now it is 14 cm × 16 cm.
2 Make a card template of a cat, and cut it out.

3   Use the template to draw a cat on a piece of black paper.

4   Cut out the cat shape and glue it on to the card front.

5   Print HALLOWE'EN over the cat.

6   Glue on two green sequins for eyes. Glue on silver stars. Write a Hallowe'en message.

Tea Party Plate

You need:

Plain paper plate, paper tissue, drinking straw, bun case, Plasticine, 2 paper cups, bit of red cellophane, glue, Sellotape.

What to do

Plate

1 Put a felt pen pattern round the edge of the plate.

2 Fold the paper tissue diagonally across in half.

3 Cut across to make a sandwich.

Cake

4   Roll a piece of Plasticine into a bun shape and stick it into the paper case.

5   Put some white glue on the bun for icing and a small ball of red tissue on top; leave it to dry. Now you have a bun to go with your sandwich.

Jelly and Cream

6   Cut off the top of the paper cup leaving a small cup.

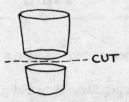

7   In this small container squash up some red cellophane (toffee paper) and glue it into the bottom.

8   Drip a little white glue on to the paper for cream.

Drink

9 Cut the next paper cup in half lengthways.

10 Sellotape the straw inside the half cup.

11 Arrange the food and drink on the plate and glue into place.

12   You might think of other food to go on the plate, or make a different kind of menu, maybe what you have had for lunch.

Ideas for other things to use as food.

Egg......polystyrene and paint.

 chips......Plasticine.

peas......green Plasticine.

 lettuce......green tissue.

spaghetti......string.

Newspaper Figures

You need:

Rolled up sheets of newspaper, scraps of material, bit of card, Sellotape, glue, felt tip pens, wool, scissors.

What to do

1 Roll up several sheets of newspaper; make long and short rolls.

2 Shape a figure with the rolls, bend a roll for the head.

3   Fasten these together really well with Sellotape.

4   Cut out a circle of card for a face, and cut out hands and feet.

5   Use wool for the hair. Glue these on to the figure.

6   Dress your figure with scraps of material; you might make a robot, a spaceman, a clown, a punk rocker or a character from your favourite story.

7   If you want to keep the figures flat, you can build up a big mural of figures for your bedroom wall and glue the figures to a large background paper.

8   When the figures are glued on and dry, paint them in bright colours.

Other ideas for a mural.

Football match   Playground

Circus   People shopping

A picnic.

Gymnastics

Two Christmas Lanterns

What to do

Lantern 1

1 Get a piece of stiff drawing paper 35 cm × 16 cm.
2 Make a colourful pattern all over with wax crayons.
3 Fold this paper in half so it is 35 cm × 8 cm.
4 Draw a line along the bottom edges 2 cm in from the
edge.

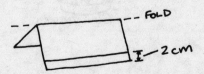

5   Cut through the FOLD down to the line all along the paper (keep the cuts narrow).

6   Unfold the paper and turn it into a roll shape; Sellotape the edge down. Squash the lantern down a little so that it bows out.

7   Draw a pattern on a strip of paper to make a handle, staple it to the top and hang up your lantern.

Lantern 2

8 Colour the top and bottom of a cardboard roll.

9 Measure a strip of paper to go round the middle of the roll, leaving a space top and bottom; fix it in place with a piece of Sellotape. This paper can be red or orange or yellow to suggest flames.

10 Cut eight strips of paper 30 cm × 2 cm, decorate each strip, colour brightly with thick wax crayons.

11 Push the ends of each strip beneath the piece of paper you have wrapped round.

12 Colour one more strip for a handle. Staple this to the top.

13 You can fasten tinsel round the top and bottom of the lantern.

14 Hang up your lantern.

Peacock Wall Mural

You need:

White drawing paper, crayons, sequins,
scissors, glue, your hand shape,
cardboard for the background.

What to do

1 Draw or trace the peacock shape. (Look on the next
page for the shape.)
2 Colour in the shape and cut it out. (Look in a book to
find the peacock's colours.)
3 On the white drawing paper draw round your hand
fourteen times and cut the shapes out.

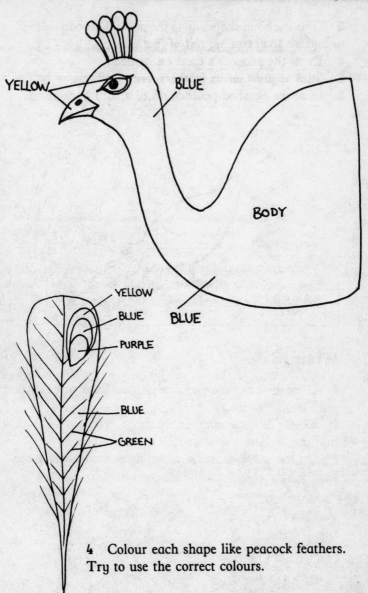

YELLOW

BLUE

BODY

YELLOW
BLUE
PURPLE

BLUE

BLUE

GREEN

4 Colour each shape like peacock feathers.
Try to use the correct colours.

5   Glue the hand shapes on to the peacock's body and tail to make a long trailing tail of feathers.

6   Draw the peacock's crest on its head.

7   Stick sequins on its feathers, crest and tail.

8   Glue the finished peacock on to a card background.

Christmas Decoration, Christmas Calendar

Different textures of wool and bright colours will add interest to this unusual decoration.

You need:

Paper plate, pencil, crayons, large-eyed darning needle, coloured wools, sequins, beads, Sellotape.

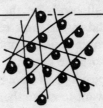

What to do

1 Use the brightest crayons to colour a design on the paper plate.
2 Poke holes with the needle all round the INSIDE rim of the plate, every 1 cm.
3 Thread the needle with coloured wool. Double the wool up and tie a knot in the end.

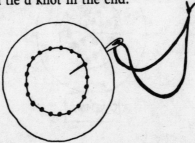

4 Start at the back of the plate, and push the needle through a hole and take the wool across to another hole, anywhere at all.

5 Do this until all the holes are taken up, then cut the thread and knot it.

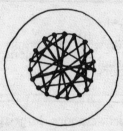

6 Tie small beads on the wool net, with tiny bits of cotton thread in the same colour as the wool.

7 Stick sequins on here and there until you have an attractive decorative design.

8 Sellotape a loop of wool behind the plate for a hanger.

9 If you want to make the plate into a calendar for the New Year, stick a calendar tab at the bottom. This is a lovely gift to use all the year round.

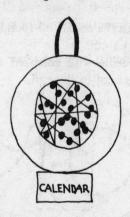

Woody Woodpecker

You need:

Stiff drawing paper
small piece 16 cm × 10 cm,
large piece 30 cm × 20 cm, crayons,
felt tip pens, scissors, 1 split pin.

What to do

1 Fold the large paper 30 cm × 20 cm down the middle.

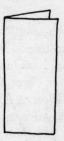

2 Cut out a V shape at the top and draw a sloping side like a tree trunk down the side. Cut a round hole in the front of the tree.

3 Colour the trunk in brown, orange and grey.

4   On the small piece of paper draw or trace the woodpecker. Colour it in black, red and white. (Look in a bird book for a woodpecker's colouring.)

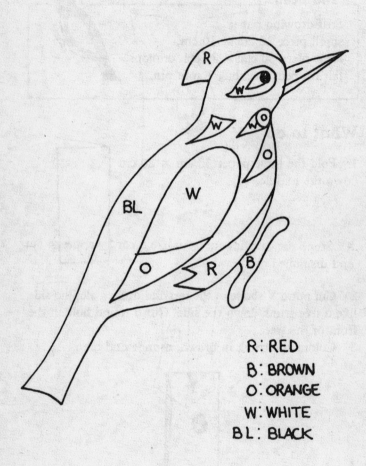

R: RED
B: BROWN
O: ORANGE
W: WHITE
BL: BLACK

5 Cut it out.
6 Put the split pin through the woodpecker and into the front of the tree.
7 Draw a nest in the hole.

8 Stand the drawing up open like a card, or spread out and displayed on the wall.

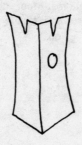

Other great reads ✦ *from* **Red Fox**

THE SNIFF STORIES Ian Whybrow

Things just keep happening to Ben Moore. It's dead hard avoiding disaster when you've got to keep your street cred with your mates *and* cope with a family of oddballs at the same time. There's his appalling 2½ year old sister, his scatty parents who are into healthy eating and animal rights and, worse than all of these, there's Sniff! If only Ben could just get on with his scientific experiments and his attempt at a world beating *Swampbeast* score . . . but there's no chance of that while chaos is just around the corner.

ISBN 0 09 9750406 £2.50

J.B. SUPERSLEUTH Joan Davenport

James Bond is a small thirteen-year-old with spots and spectacles. But with a name like that, how can he help being a supersleuth?

It all started when James and 'Polly' (Paul) Perkins spotted a teacher's stolen car. After that, more and more mysteries needed solving. With the case of the Arabian prince, the Murdered Model, the Bonfire Night Murder and the Lost Umbrella, JB's reputation at Moorside Comprehensive soars.

But some of the cases aren't quite what they seem . . .

ISBN 0 09 9717808 £1.99